The Business Sellers Guide

Strategies For A Successful Exit

2024 Edition

Craig Bartlett

The Business Seller's Guide: Strategies for a Successful Exit
(2024 Edition)

Introduction
- The various reasons why business owners decide to sell.
- Overview of the current UK business sales environment in 2024 (economic state, regulations, trends in buyer interest).
- Dispelling common misconceptions about selling a business.

Chapter 1: Is Selling Your Business the Right Decision?
- Emotional vs. practical considerations
- Identifying realistic personal and financial goals for the sale.
- Analysing alternatives to selling (e.g., handing over to family, retaining with a hired manager, etc.).
- Determining the optimal timeline for selling.

Chapter 2: Maximising Your Business's Valuation
- Key factors influencing business valuation (profitability, growth prospects, assets, etc.).
- Pre-sale cleanup: Improving financials, organisation, and legal compliance.
- Finding comparable business sales to estimate realistic worth.
- The role of professional valuators and how to find one.

Chapter 3: Understanding the Tax Implications
- Short-term and long-term capital gains considerations.
- Entrepreneurs' Relief and other potential tax breaks.
- Strategies for pre- and post-sale tax planning.
- The importance of working with a UK tax professional.

Chapter 4: Preparing Your Business for Sale
- Creating a compelling business profile/information memorandum.
- Organising essential documentation (financials, contracts, etc.).
- Addressing any red flags or potential buyer concerns proactively.
- The art of "staging" your business for maximum appeal.

Chapter 5: Finding the Right Buyer
- Private sales vs. working with brokers.
- Using online marketplaces and business-for-sale websites in the UK.
- Strategically networking to find potential buyers.
- Evaluating different types of buyers (individuals, competitors, investment groups).

Chapter 6: The Art of Negotiation
- Setting realistic expectations on price and terms.
- Developing a negotiation strategy and understanding your BATNA (Best Alternative to a Negotiated Agreement).
- Anticipating buyer tactics and due diligence questions.
- Using non-disclosure agreements (NDAs) effectively.

Chapter 7: Structuring the Deal

- Common deal structures (asset vs. share purchase).
- Understanding earn-outs, seller financing, and other payment mechanisms.
- The importance of clear contracts and legal representation.
- Navigating due diligence and common pitfalls.

Chapter 8: Transition and Handover
- Creating a seamless transition plan for employees, clients, and operations.
- Seller's role post-sale: Consulting, non-compete agreements, etc.
- Strategies for protecting intellectual property and trade secrets.
- Emotional preparedness for letting go.

Chapter 9: Life After the Sale
- Managing wealth and financial planning.
- Avoiding common pitfalls of sudden wealth.
- Exploring new opportunities – entrepreneurship, investment, or enjoying retirement.
- Finding purpose and staying engaged beyond work.

Chapter 10: Case Studies
- Success stories of business sales in the UK (examples from diverse industries).
- Lessons learned and common mistakes to avoid.

Conclusion
- Summarises key takeaways, emphasising the importance of planning.
- Encouragement for a successful and personally fulfilling exit.

Foreword From Author: Craig Bartlett

I have been an "Entrepreneur" for most of my life - and prior to becoming involved with mergers and acquisitions, I'm proud to say that I successfully negotiated the sale of multiple businesses. It was only in more recent years, however, that I realised how many good small and medium-sized businesses that are advertised for sale, never actually sell. There's many reasons for this - but the two most frequent are: 1) Underprepared or unrealistic owners, and 2) Poor or misleading representation on behalf of the owners.

Having been a small business owner myself, it's devastating to hear that approximately 80% of businesses don't actually sell. That's 4 out of 5! All those years of dedication and hard work with no reward at the end. So I found my "why" - and that is to help SMB owners - when they are growing their businesses, when they are planning an exit, and when they are actively selling.

I hope this short book helps to prepare SMB owners for the journey ahead - and that you can then achieve the reward for which all your hard work deserves.

Introduction

Selling your business is a momentous decision. It represents the culmination of years, perhaps decades, of hard work, risk-taking, and relentless dedication. Whether you're dreaming of a well-deserved retirement, seeking new entrepreneurial ventures, or simply facing changing life circumstances, deciding to exit your business is a move fraught with both excitement and uncertainty.

The UK business sales landscape is constantly evolving. In 2024, economic conditions, regulatory shifts, and evolving buyer preferences all play significant roles in shaping successful sales. This book is your guide to navigating this dynamic environment with confidence, maximising the value of your hard-earned business, and preparing yourself for a fulfilling next chapter.

We'll dispel the myths and misunderstandings about selling a business. You'll gain the tools to honestly assess whether selling is the right path, establish your goals, and create a timeline that works for you. We'll delve into valuation, preparing your business to shine, and attracting the ideal buyer – all while considering the vital tax implications of a UK business sale.

This book isn't just about financials; it's about you, the business owner. We'll address the emotional complexities involved in letting go, transitioning the business you've poured yourself into, and planning for a purpose-filled life after the sale.
Think of this guide as a trusted advisor. It blends practical steps with real-world insights from successful sellers, brokers, and specialists – empowering you to sell your business in the UK strategically, profitably, and with peace of mind.

Let's get started.

Chapter 1: Is Selling Your Business the Right Decision?

The idea of selling your business has been swirling in your mind. Perhaps it's a fleeting thought sparked by a tempting offer, or a persistent itch as you begin to dream about life's next chapter. Regardless of the trigger, deciding to sell a business you've built is rarely a simple yes or no answer.

This chapter is about honest self-evaluation. It's about separating practical considerations from the emotional weight often entwined with entrepreneurship. We'll examine the compelling reasons why owners choose to sell, while also considering viable alternatives. By the end of this chapter, you'll gain the clarity to determine whether selling is genuinely the right path for you at this specific time.

Why Do People Sell Their Businesses?

- **Retirement:** Perhaps the most common reason, especially for founders nearing traditional retirement age. Selling provides financial security and the freedom to pursue new interests.
- **New Ventures:** Your entrepreneurial spirit is itching for a fresh challenge. Selling your current business frees up capital and energy for new pursuits.
- **Burnout:** The demands of running a business can take a toll. If you're facing diminishing passion and increasing stress, selling could be a way to regain balance.
- **Changing Life Circumstances:** Unexpected health issues, family needs, or simply a desire for a major lifestyle change may make continuing as an owner untenable.
- **Unsolicited Offer:** An attractive offer can be tempting, even if selling wasn't previously on your radar. It's essential to weigh it carefully, rather than acting impulsively.

Beyond the Obvious: Emotional Considerations

Selling a business is like giving up part of your identity. Your company may embody years of sacrifice, triumphs, and perhaps even failures that shaped you. Acknowledging these emotions is crucial.

Ask yourself:

- Is my ego tied to being the business owner?
- Am I afraid of what life will be like without the business?
- Do I feel guilty potentially affecting employees' lives?

Consulting with a trusted business advisor or even a therapist can help process these complex feelings.

Alternatives to Selling

It's wise to explore other options before committing to a full sale:

- **Handing Over to Family:** Is there a next generation interested and capable of taking on ownership?
- **Hiring a Professional Manager:** Could outsourcing daily operations allow you to step back without a full exit?

- **Partial Sale:** If you desire a less drastic change, consider selling a stake in the business while retaining some ownership.

Crafting Your Goals

Whether you ultimately decide to sell or pursue an alternative, clearly defining your goals is essential. Consider:

- **Financial Needs:** What level of after-tax proceeds do you require to live the lifestyle you desire?
- **Legacy:** Is preserving your business's name and community impact important to you?
- **Timeline:** Do you have a hard deadline (e.g., pending move), or a more flexible time frame for a sale?

The Importance of Timing

Selling a business under duress, be it financial strain or personal health crises, rarely results in an optimal outcome. Starting this process proactively ensures you have the time to consider all options and position your business for the best sale.

Key Takeaways

- The decision to sell a business is both deeply personal and financially complex.
- Honest self-examination about your motivations and goals is essential.
- There may be viable alternatives to a full sale.
- Proactive planning leads to better outcomes than rushed decisions.

By taking the time for this thoughtful analysis, you'll pave the way for a confident decision – whether it's putting a "For Sale" sign up or reinvigorating your business with renewed purpose.

Chapter 2: Maximising Your Business's Valuation

Picture this: You've spent years building a profitable business, and now it's time to sell. You might naturally assume potential buyers will immediately recognize its inherent worth and line up with generous offers. Unfortunately, business valuation rarely works that way. Maximising the sale price of your business requires a strategic approach. In this chapter, we'll unpack the key factors that influence valuation, discuss actions you can take to improve your business's value before listing, and demystify the role of professional valuation services.

What Drives Valuation?

Think of potential buyers as investors seeking a return on investment. Key aspects they consider include:

- **Profitability:** It reigns supreme. Your business's ability to generate consistent and growing profits is the core driver of value. This includes both topline revenue and a healthy bottom-line (net profit).
- **Growth Potential:** Stagnation isn't appealing. Buyers look for businesses with a track record of growth and a clear roadmap for future expansion.
- **Assets:** Tangible assets (equipment, property) and intangible assets (patents, trademarks) contribute to valuation.
- **Risk Profile:** Businesses with predictable revenue streams, strong customer bases, and few significant threats are deemed less risky and thus, more valuable.

Pre-Sale Cleanup: Improve Your Bottom Line

Before listing your business, take these steps:

- **Optimise Financials:** Review profit and loss statements and balance sheets. Spot opportunities to cut costs, increase revenue, and tidy up financial presentation.
- **Organise Documentation:** Gather tax returns, business licences, contracts, and client agreements. A well-organised business is an attractive one.
- **Address Legal Issues:** Resolve outstanding legal disputes or looming compliance risks that might deter buyers.
- **Streamline Operations:** Can any processes be made more efficient to reduce reliance on the owner's direct involvement?

Comparable Sales: Finding a Realistic Benchmark

Investigate recent sales of businesses similar to yours in size, sector, and geographical location. This data, often available through industry associations or business brokers, provides valuable reference points. Be cautious of overestimating your business's value based on outliers; focus on realistic comparisons.

Should You Hire a Business Valuator?

For larger or complex businesses, a professional valuation provides several benefits:

- **Credibility:** A third-party valuation lends legitimacy to your asking price.

- **Negotiation Power:** A detailed valuation report gives you solid data to back up your position.
- **Reveal Hidden Value:** Valuators may identify overlooked intangible assets or factors boosting your valuation.

Methods of Valuation

Three main methods are commonly used:

- **Asset-based:** Assesses the fair market value of assets minus liabilities. This approach is often a minimum valuation floor.
- **Income-based:** Uses discounted cash flow or a multiple of earnings (e.g., EBITDA) to project future profitability.
- **Market-based** Leverages sales data of comparable businesses as a valuation benchmark.

Key Takeaways

- Business valuation is part science, part art. Buyers prioritise profitability and growth.
- Taking steps to optimise your business before a sale can significantly increase its value.
- Comparable sales data provides a reality check for your expectations.
- Professional valuation services add credibility and may reveal overlooked value drivers.

Maximising valuation isn't just about the final number. It's about demonstrating to potential buyers that your business is a sound and promising investment, worthy of their hard-earned money.

Chapter 3: Understanding the Tax Implications

The thrill of potentially selling your business can quickly fade when faced with the complexities of UK tax law. Understanding the tax implications of a sale is absolutely crucial to ensure you maximise your financial gains and avoid unwelcome surprises post-sale.

In this chapter, we'll demystify the basics of business sale taxation, highlighting potential tax-saving opportunities and the importance of expert advice.

Capital Gains Tax (CGT)

The bulk of your business sale proceeds will likely be subject to Capital Gains Tax. The specific rate of CGT you pay depends on your personal income tax bracket and whether you qualify for certain reliefs, discussed next.

Entrepreneurs' Relief

This incredibly valuable relief can significantly reduce your tax bill. To qualify, you and your business must meet several criteria:

- You are a shareholder or employee holding at least 5% of the company's shares.
- The company is a trading company (not primarily investment-focused).
- You've held the shares for at least two years prior to the sale.

Entrepreneurs' Relief currently offers a lifetime allowance of £1 million in reduced-rate CGT (10%). Utilising this relief wisely is a vital part of tax planning.

Other Potential Tax Considerations

- **Rollover Relief:** Reinvesting sale proceeds into a new business venture may allow you to defer CGT payment.
- **Inheritance Tax:** Planning ahead can help to minimise inheritance tax exposure if the business forms part of your estate.
- **Stamp Duty:** This tax may apply on the transfer of certain assets, such as property.

Navigating Complexities: Why You Need a Tax Specialist

The UK tax code is notoriously intricate, and the rules around business sales are no exception. A tax advisor specialising in business transactions will:

- Assess your eligibility for Entrepreneurs' Relief and other tax breaks.
- Structure the deal to minimise tax liabilities.
- Plan proactively for pre- and post-sale tax scenarios.
- Handle HMRC reporting and compliance on your behalf.

Pre-Sale Tax Planning

Consulting a tax advisor early in the selling process can be a game-changer. They might suggest strategies like:

- **Timing the Sale:** Strategically timing the sale of your business to take advantage of different tax years and allowances.
- **Maximising Deductions:** Ensuring all eligible business expenses are claimed before the sale to reduce your taxable profits.

Post-Sale Planning

How you manage the sales proceeds can significantly impact your future tax liability. A financial advisor in tandem with your tax advisor can offer guidance on:

- **Investment Strategies:** Investing wisely for both income generation and tax efficiency.
- **Gifting:** Strategically gifting some proceeds to reduce potential inheritance tax burdens.
- **Pension Contributions:** Utilising pensions as a tax-efficient means of wealth management.

Key Takeaways

- Business sale taxation in the UK is complex and requires specialist advice.
- Proactive tax planning can significantly reduce your tax burden and maximise profits.
- Entrepreneurs' Relief is a game-changer, and understanding its rules is key.
- Post-sale financial planning is just as crucial as pre-sale tax strategy.

Don't let taxes erode your hard-earned profits. A savvy approach to taxation can turn a good business deal into an exceptional one.

Chapter 4: Preparing Your Business for Sale

Think of your business as a house you're putting on the market. It may have strong bones, but curb appeal matters. This chapter is about making your business shine to attract the most qualified buyers – and secure the best possible price.

Crafting Your Business Profile

Your business profile, or information memorandum, is a crucial sales tool. It paints a detailed picture of your business, not just the numbers, but also the story. Include:

- **Company Overview:** History, mission, value proposition, market niche, competitive advantages.
- **Financials:** Three to five years of audited income statements, cash flow statements, and balance sheets. Include projections with clear assumptions.
- **Operations:** Management structure, key employees, processes and systems, customer profiles.
- **Growth Potential:** Expansion plans, new market opportunities, untapped revenue streams.
- **Intangible Assets:** Intellectual property, brand recognition, customer loyalty.

The Art of Presentation

- **Professionalism Counts:** A polished layout, error-free writing, and high-quality visuals enhance credibility.
- **Confidentiality is Key:** Use non-disclosure agreements (NDAs) to protect sensitive information.
- **Tell Your Story:** Weave in a narrative of the business's journey, highlighting its unique strengths and potential. Be passionate without being unrealistic.

Addressing Red Flags

Anticipate buyer concerns and tackle them preemptively:

- **Customer Concentration:** Is revenue dependent on a few large clients? Highlight strategies to diversify your customer base.
- **Owner Reliance:** Is your business too reliant on your personal involvement? Document systems and procedures, showing a potential buyer how it can run smoothly without you.
- **Outdated Technology:** Has investment in tech kept pace with industry needs? Outline upgrades if necessary.

Staging Your Business

Just as you would declutter and deep-clean your home before a showing, take these steps:

- **Boost Curb Appeal:** Small enhancements to your premises or website can create a positive first impression.
- **Optimise Online Presence:** Ensure your website is up-to-date and SEO optimised to attract online interest.
- **Gather Documentation:** Organise contracts, licences, and other legal documents in a

clear and accessible manner.

Should You Hire a Business Broker?

Especially for larger or complex businesses, brokers offer:

- **Valuation Guidance:** Setting realistic expectations for sale price.
- **Preparation Assistance:** Helping to create a compelling business profile.
- **Finding Buyers:** Access to their network and online marketplace advertising.
- **Confidentiality Management:** Protecting sensitive information during the process.

Key Takeaways

- Investing time and effort into presentation maximises your business's appeal.
- Your business profile is more than numbers – it's the story of your business.
- Addressing any potential red flags proactively strengthens your negotiating position.
- "Staging" your business can leave a lasting positive impression on buyers.

By turning your business into its most attractive self, you'll create heightened buyer interest—the foundation for a successful and profitable sale.

Chapter 5: Finding the Right Buyer

You've meticulously prepared your business for sale – now it's time to find the ideal buyer. It's about more than just the highest offer; finding a buyer whose vision aligns with your values, who appreciates your employees, and who plans to take your business to even greater heights often leads to a smoother sale and a more satisfying outcome for everyone involved.

The Search Strategies

Let's explore various avenues to connect with potential buyers:

- **Business Brokers:** Experienced brokers have an existing network of potential buyers, know the sales process inside out, and can handle marketing and negotiations on your behalf.
- **Online Marketplaces:** Websites specialising in business sales (e.g. BusinessesForSale.com & RightBiz.co.uk offer increased exposure but often necessitate more due diligence to determine serious buyers.
- **Direct Outreach:** Target competitors, suppliers, or companies in a complementary industry for whom your business may be a strategic acquisition.
- **Industry Networks:** Utilise trade associations, conferences, and your professional network to discreetly spread the word that your business is for sale.
- **Your Employees:** Is there a possibility of a management buyout? Sometimes the right buyer may be closer than you think.

Types of Buyers

Understanding who is looking to buy businesses like yours is key:

- **Individual Investors:** Entrepreneurs seeking to own and operate a business.
- **Larger Companies:** Acquiring your business may be part of their growth strategy.
- **Private Equity Firms:** Investment groups focused on purchasing businesses and typically implementing changes to increase value.

Qualifying Potential Buyers

Not all interest means suitable offers. Pre-screening saves time and frustration by ensuring:

- **Financial Capacity:** Can they realistically afford your business? Ask for proof of funds or pre-approval letters.
- **Relevant Experience:** Do they possess the industry knowledge or business acumen to successfully run the company?
- **Shared Vision:** Are their plans for your business's future in line with your preferences?

Non-Disclosure Agreements (NDAs)

Always have a detailed and enforceable NDA in place before sharing sensitive business information. Consult with your solicitor to ensure it adequately protects your interests.

Key Takeaways

- Finding the right buyer enhances the chances of a smooth sale and successful transition.
- A mix of proactive and discreet strategies can maximise buyer reach.
- Don't underestimate the power of your existing network.
- Evaluate potential buyers based on financial capacity, experience, and alignment with your vision.
- NDAs are non-negotiable to protect your confidential business information.

The ideal buyer will see the inherent value in your business, pay a fair price, and set the stage for your business's continued growth under new leadership.

Important questions to ask potential buyers:

Financial Capacity

- How do you plan to finance the purchase? (Cash, loan, a mix?)
- Can you provide proof of funds, a pre-approval letter, or financial statements to demonstrate your financial capacity?
- Are there any contingencies related to financing that could delay or jeopardise the deal?

Experience and Motivation

- What is your experience in owning or managing businesses, especially in this industry?
- Why are you interested in acquiring our business specifically?
- What are your short- and long-term goals for the business?

Vision and Operations

- Do you intend to make significant changes to operations, staffing, or product/service offerings?
- How do you see yourself integrating the business into your existing operations (if applicable)?
- What is your approach to managing employees and company culture?

Specific to Your Priorities

- If legacy is important: Are you committed to preserving the business name and reputation in the community?
- If employees are a concern: What are your plans regarding the existing workforce?
- If you desire a quick exit: Are you prepared to move quickly through due diligence and the closing process?

Additional Tips

- **Listen closely:** Pay attention to how they answer and anything that may raise red flags.
- **Don't be afraid to ask follow-up questions:** Probe deeper to get clarity on any vague responses.
- **Consider a written questionnaire:** This ensures consistency for comparing multiple buyers.
- **Trust your gut:** Sometimes intuition plays a role in discerning serious buyers versus those simply window shopping.

Extra Considerations:

The type of buyer may make additional questions necessary. For example:

- **With strategic buyers (e.g., competitors):** What synergies do you envision between our businesses? Are there any potential antitrust concerns?
- **With private equity:** What is your typical investment timeline and exit strategy?

By asking thoughtful, targeted questions, you'll gain the insights needed to confidently identify the buyer who is most likely to offer you a fair price, ensure a smooth transition, and take your business to the next level of success.

Buyer Behavior Red Flags:

- **Excessive Pressure Tactics:** A buyer who constantly pushes for tight deadlines, lowball offers, or unreasonable concessions might be desperate to close the deal quickly, potentially to cover up underlying problems.
- **Frequent Changes in Terms:** A buyer who keeps changing their mind on key deal points, especially after seemingly reaching an agreement, could be disorganised or have hidden agendas.
- **Lack of Transparency:** A buyer who hesitates to share information about their financing, future plans for the business, or their own company's background could be hiding something.

Due Diligence Red Flags:

- **Unexplained Discrepancies:** Unforeseen inconsistencies in the buyer's financial statements or business history could indicate financial instability or a history of troubled ventures.
- **Excessive Focus on Unimportant Issues:** A buyer who spends an unreasonable amount of time nitpicking minor details in due diligence might be trying to find a reason to walk away or renegotiate the price downwards.
- **Walking Away from Negotiations Abruptly:** If a buyer exits negotiations abruptly over seemingly small issues, it could be a sign they weren't serious to begin with, or that they have uncovered a major undisclosed problem.

Legal and Financial Red Flags:

- **Vague or Unrealistic Financing Plans:** A buyer relying on uncertain financing sources or offering overly complex financing structures could be at risk of falling

through on the deal at the last minute.
- **History of Lawsuits:** If the buyer has a history of legal issues, particularly involving fraud or failure to meet contractual obligations, it's a cause for concern.
- **Unwillingness to Address Liabilities:** A buyer hesitant to acknowledge or take responsibility for potential business liabilities might be hoping to shift those burdens onto you after the sale.

Remember: It's always better to walk away from a bad deal than to get locked into an agreement with a buyer who could create problems down the road. Trust your gut, and don't be afraid to raise concerns with your legal team if any of these red flags appear.

Chapter 6: The Art of Negotiation

Selling a business is rarely a "take-it-or-leave-it" scenario. This chapter is about honing your negotiation skills, understanding buyer tactics, and coming away from the negotiation table confident that you achieved the best possible outcome.

Preparation is Power

- **Set Your BATNA:** Know your "Best Alternative to a Negotiated Agreement." What's the absolute minimum you'd accept, and what would you do if negotiations fail?
- **Know Your Walk-Away Point:** Determine beforehand the price below which you'll refuse an offer.
- **Understand Your Leverage:** Are there multiple interested buyers? Does your business possess unique advantages that make it more desirable?
- **Anticipate Buyer Questions:** Prepare well-reasoned responses about financials, growth potential, and any areas they may probe during due diligence.

The Offer and Counteroffer

The initial offer is often below your asking price. Here's how to handle it:

- **Stay Calm:** Avoid emotional reactions. Consider it the opening move in a strategic dance.
- **Analyse Beyond Price:** Are the proposed deal terms (payment structure, contingencies) favourable?
- **Counteroffer Strategically:** Don't just split the difference. Use data and persuasive arguments to support your counteroffer.

Common Buyer Tactics

- **Lowball Offer:** Designed to test your resolve. Hold firm to your valuation.
- **"Nitpicking" During Due Diligence:** Some issues may be genuine concerns, while others may be used to chip away at price. Distinguish between the two.
- **Last-Minute Pressure:** Don't be rushed into a hasty decision. If a deadline seems artificial, call their bluff.

Beyond the Price Tag: Negotiating Deal Terms

- **Earn-Outs:** Consider an earn-out structure if the buyer's growth projections seem overly optimistic. This ties part of the payment to future business performance.
- **Seller Financing:** Offering to finance part of the sale can make your business more attractive to some buyers.
- **Consulting Period:** Your expertise can be valuable during a transition. Negotiate a consulting agreement if appropriate.

Protecting Yourself

- **Legal Counsel is Key:** Have your solicitor review any Letter of Intent and the final purchase agreement.

- **Due Diligence Goes Both Ways:** Investigate the buyer's financial resources and reputation.
- **No Verbal Agreements:** Get everything in writing to avoid misunderstandings later.

Key Takeaways

- Negotiating a business sale is a process, not a single event.
- Strength comes from understanding your value and having a clear walk-away point.
- Focus on the overall deal structure, not just the final sale price.
- Seek professional advice to ensure your interests are protected.

Successful negotiation is both about maximising financial gains and ensuring a deal that leaves you feeling satisfied knowing you've passed on your business to responsible hands.

Chapter 7: Structuring the Deal

Congratulations! You've reached an agreement on price and major terms. Now it's time to translate that into a legally binding purchase agreement – where the details truly matter. Understanding deal structures, navigating the complexities of due diligence, and working closely with your legal team are paramount to safeguarding your interests and avoiding costly pitfalls.

Deal Structures: Asset Purchase vs. Share Purchase

- **Asset Purchase:** The buyer acquires specific business assets (equipment, inventory, customer contracts), usually offering the seller some liability protection.
- **Share Purchase:** The buyer acquires ownership of the entire company, including assets and any unknown liabilities. This is often simpler but riskier for the seller.

The Importance of Clear Contracts

Never rely on a handshake. Your purchase agreement should meticulously define:

- **Assets Included:** List everything transferred, especially intangibles like patents and website domain.
- **Payment Terms:** Amount, instalments, earn-outs, seller financing details (interest rates, repayment period).
- **Representations and Warranties:** Statements both you and the buyer make about the business's state.
- **Non-Compete Agreements:** Prevent you from starting a competing business too soon or in the same area.
- **Contingencies:** Conditions that must be met for closing (e.g., financing secured, regulatory approval).

Due Diligence: The Buyer's Deep Dive

Expect the buyer to scrutinise your business. Be prepared to provide:

- **Detailed Financials:** Income statements, balance sheets, tax returns, bank records.
- **Legal Documentation:** Contracts, leases, licences, intellectual property filings.
- **Customer & Supplier Information:** Sales contracts, major customer lists.
- **Employee Data:** Payroll records, benefits agreements, organisational charts.

Protecting Yourself During Due Diligence

- **Data Room:** Utilise a secure online data room to control access to sensitive information.
- **Work with Your Solicitor:** They ensure what's requested is reasonable and confidential documents are protected.
- **Anticipate Red Flags:** Address potential issues uncovered during due diligence proactively.

Common Pitfalls and Red Flags

- **Inadequate Due Diligence:** If the buyer isn't thorough, you could face post-sale lawsuits.
- **Unrealistic Earn-Outs:** Ensure earn-out terms are achievable and measurable.
- **Overly Restrictive Non-Compete:** Negotiate reasonable limits on your future business activities.

Key Takeaways

- The specifics of your deal's structure and contract terms have long-term implications.
- Proactive due diligence preparation streamlines the process and minimises surprises.
- Your solicitor is your strongest ally in ensuring the contract protects your interests.
- Don't underestimate the impact of deal terms on your post-sale financial position and future endeavours.

While the finish line might seem in sight, signing the purchase agreement is a means to an end – the successful closing of the sale and receipt of your hard-earned proceeds.

Chapter 8: Transition and Handover

Closing day is a milestone, but it's not the end of your involvement in the business you've built. A successful transition ensures your company's continued success, protects your legacy, and allows you to confidently step away.

Create a Transition Plan

Work with the buyer to outline:

- **Knowledge Transfer:** Document key processes, systems, client relationships, and industry-specific information.
- **Employee Handoff:** Clearly communicate changes to employees. If key employees are leaving, help with the hiring process of their replacements.
- **Customer Communication:** Jointly create a handover plan to reassure clients and maintain trust.
- **Timeline:** Phase out your involvement gradually if possible, providing mentorship as needed.

The Role of Post-Sale Consulting

- **Formalise the Agreement:** If providing post-sale consulting, negotiate hourly rates, time commitment, and specific deliverables as a separate agreement.
- **Advantages:** Consulting can ease the transition, maintain goodwill with the buyer, and provide extra income.
- **Potential Pitfalls:** Avoid getting drawn into daily operations indefinitely, set clear boundaries.

Protecting Your Intellectual Property

- **Patents & Trademarks:** Ensure proper transfer or licensing agreements are in place if these are part of the sale.
- **Trade Secrets:** Formalise non-disclosure agreements for any proprietary knowledge you retain.
- **Brand Reputation:** Consider negotiating veto rights over major branding or marketing changes that could damage your legacy.

Emotional Readiness

It's natural to feel mixed emotions when handing over the business you've poured yourself into. Here's how to cope:

- **Have a Plan:** Focus on new goals or ventures you'll pursue post-sale.
- **Don't Look Back:** Avoid second-guessing decisions or constantly comparing your leadership to the new owner's.
- **Celebrate Your Achievements:** Take pride in what you built and the opportunity you've created for yourself and others.
- **Seek Support:** Talk to trusted advisors, mentors, or even a therapist if needed to process feelings of loss.

Key Takeaways

- A well-planned transition ensures your business thrives under new ownership.
- Consulting agreements can provide continuity but require clear boundaries.
- Proactively protect your intellectual property and intangible contributions to the business.
- Emotional preparedness is as important as any business document for a fulfilling exit.

Letting go is never easy, but by focusing on your next chapter and trusting you've done everything possible to set up the business and its new owners for success, you can embrace the exciting possibilities that lie ahead.

Sample Transition Plan Outline

This is a general outline, and you can customise it based on the specifics of your business and the buyer's needs.

I. Introduction

- Briefly state the purpose of the transition plan.
- Outline the timeframe for the transition process.
- Identify key personnel involved from both the seller and buyer sides.

II. Knowledge Transfer

- **A. Core Business Operations:**
  - List critical processes and standard operating procedures (SOPs) to be documented and transferred to the buyer (e.g., sales process, customer service protocols, inventory management).
  - Identify the personnel responsible for creating the documentation and training the buyer's team.
- **B. Customer Management:**
  - Plan a communication strategy to inform customers about the ownership change.
  - Determine how customer information and account management will be transitioned.
- **C. Technology and Systems:**
  - Create a detailed inventory of hardware, software, and any relevant IT systems.
  - Develop a handover plan for passwords, access rights, and ongoing technical support (if applicable).
- **D. Legal and Compliance:**
  - Identify all essential licences, permits, and contracts that need to be reviewed and transferred to the new ownership.
  - Outline a process for ensuring ongoing compliance with regulations.

III. Employee Transition

- Develop a communication plan for announcing the sale to employees.
- Identify any employee introductions or training sessions needed with the new owner.
- If there are personnel changes, establish a clear severance or outplacement plan (if

applicable).
- Determine how benefits and payroll will be handled during the transition period.

IV. Inventory Management

- Establish a procedure for inventory handover, including stock counts and valuation.
- Determine how any ongoing purchase orders or supplier relationships will be transitioned.

V. Post-Sale Support (Optional)

- Outline the terms of any consulting agreement if the seller will be providing ongoing guidance.
- Define clear communication channels and protocols for post-sale support.

VI. Timeline and Milestones

- Create a detailed timeline with milestones for each key activity in the transition plan.
- Assign ownership for completing each task.

VII. Contingency Plans

- Identify potential roadblocks or unforeseen circumstances that could arise during the transition.
- Develop contingency plans to address these situations.

VIII. Communication Plan

- Establish clear communication channels between the seller, buyer, and employees throughout the transition.
- Determine the frequency and format of communication updates.

IX. Review and Approval

- Both the buyer and seller should review and approve the final transition plan.

X. Revisions

- Acknowledge that the plan may need to be revised as the handover progresses.

Chapter 9: Life After the Sale

You've signed the final documents and received the proceeds from selling your business. Now what? This chapter is about smart financial management, avoiding pitfalls of sudden wealth, and discovering new passions to create a fulfilling new chapter in your life.

Managing Your Wealth

- **Professional Guidance:** A financial advisor specialising in wealth management can help you develop a comprehensive plan.
- **Investment Strategy:** Create a diversified portfolio that aligns with your risk tolerance and long-term goals.
- **Tax Planning:** Strategize with your accountant to minimise tax burdens on your sale proceeds.
- **Estate Planning:** Update wills, trusts, and life insurance policies to reflect your changed financial situation.

Common Mistakes to Avoid

- **Impulsive Spending:** Resist the urge to splurge. Give yourself time to adjust to your newfound wealth before major purchases.
- **Risky Investments:** Don't be lured by get-rich-quick schemes. Stick to a sound, diversified investment plan.
- **Failing to Budget:** Even with greater wealth, a budget ensures your lifestyle is sustainable long-term.
- **Neglecting Philanthropy:** If charitable giving is important, establish a structured plan to make meaningful contributions.

Finding Purpose Beyond Work

Many entrepreneurs struggle when their identity is no longer intertwined with their business. Here's how to proactively create a fulfilling future:

- **Explore Interests:** What did you always want to do but lacked time for? Travel, hobbies, volunteering, learning a new skill?
- **Mentorship:** Share your knowledge by mentoring aspiring entrepreneurs or serving on non-profit boards.
- **Angel Investing:** Support the next generation of startups and potentially find new meaning in helping others succeed.
- **New Business Ventures:** Does the sale spark ideas for another, perhaps smaller-scale, business venture?
- **Give Back:** Consider dedicating time and resources to a cause you care deeply about.

The Importance of Community

- **Avoid Isolation:** Maintain your social network or connect with communities of retired or semi-retired entrepreneurs.
- **Embrace New Experiences:** Take classes, join clubs, or travel groups to forge new connections and uncover hidden interests.

- **Focus on Wellbeing:** Prioritise both physical and mental health. Having time for wellness is a perk of a successful exit.

Key Takeaways

- Your wealth from the sale is a tool for creating the life you truly want.
- Financial planning and discipline are key to ensuring your money works for you long-term.
- Rediscovering your passions and reinventing your sense of purpose are essential for a fulfilling post-business life.
- Don't underestimate the power of community in navigating your next chapter.

Selling your business is the end of one era but the exciting beginning of another. Invest in planning, explore new possibilities, and embrace this opportunity to design an extraordinary life both financially and personally.

Chapter 10: Case Studies and Expert Insights

In this chapter, we move from theory to practice. Stories of real business sales provide valuable context, inspire solutions to common challenges, and spotlight the expert wisdom that has guided us through this book.

Success Stories

Let's showcase 3 diverse businesses from the UK:

- **Family-Owned Manufacturing Business:** Illustrating navigating emotional attachment and ensuring a legacy for employees.
- **A Well Established Recruitment Sole Proprietorship:** Highlighting changing markets and the founder's transition journey.
- **Small, Local Business:** Demonstrating the importance of valuing customer relationships and documenting intangible assets.

Each case study will include:

- Company context & reasons for selling
- Key challenges the seller faced
- Strategies that led to a favourable outcome
- Seller's reflections on life after the sale

Lessons Learned and Common Mistakes

We'll distil key themes across case studies::

- **Time = Money:** Emphasise that proactive preparation often equates to a higher sale price and smoother transition.
- **It's Never Just About the Price:** Highlight the importance of the buyer's vision, employee considerations, and the seller's post-sale plans.
- **Beware of These Red Flags:** Reinforce potential pitfalls in the negotiation and due diligence phases.

Case Study: Precision Metalworks Ltd.

- **Industry:** Precision metal fabrication (automotive components)
- **Location:** Midlands, UK
- **Business Structure:** Family-owned, operated for 35 years
- **Reason for Selling:** Founder nearing retirement, no interested heirs within the family. Desire to secure the future of long-term employees.

Challenges:

- **Emotional Attachment:** The founder built the business from scratch. Letting go triggered mixed feelings of pride and trepidation about life beyond work.
- **Valuation Concerns:** Recent fluctuations in raw material pricing raised questions about the company's accurate valuation and potential impact on the sale price.
- **Employee Uncertainty:** Employees were anxious about their jobs under new ownership and potential disruptions to their workflow/company culture.

Strategies for Success:

- **Professional Valuation:** A business valuation specialist provided a well-reasoned assessment that helped the seller set realistic expectations and gave potential buyers confidence in the company's value.
- **Emphasis on Skilled Workforce:** The business profile showcased the experience and loyalty of the company's machinists and support staff, emphasising this as an essential asset.
- **Proactive Communication:** The seller openly addressed employee concerns, highlighting his priority of finding a buyer who appreciated their value and would retain the existing team.

Outcome:

Precision Metalworks was acquired by a mid-sized manufacturing enterprise seeking to expand its capabilities. The purchase included:

- A 5-year consulting agreement with the founder to ensure smooth knowledge transfer.
- Employee retention bonuses and long-term contracts for key staff.
- The original founder, on reflection, expressed relief that his legacy continues and he established a comfortable retirement alongside a newfound passion for mentoring apprentices in the manufacturing field.

Lessons Learned:

- Even in asset-heavy industries, the human element (workforce, founder's knowledge) can be major drivers of value.
- Addressing the emotional side of a sale can ease transitions and attract buyers who prioritise a company's culture.
- Post-sale consulting agreements can be a win-win, providing the seller with income and purpose while ensuring a smooth handover.

Case Study: TalentFinders Recruitment Agency

- **Industry:** Recruitment (specialising in IT & finance professionals)
- **Location:** London, UK
- **Business Structure:** Sole proprietorship, operating for 12 years
- **Reason for Selling:** Burnout and desire for a career change. The owner felt increasing competition from online recruitment platforms was eroding margins.

Challenges:

- **Intangible Assets:** The business's primary assets were the owner's network of candidates and clients, and her industry reputation. Quantifying this value was challenging.
- **Client Retention Concerns:** Clients were often loyal to the owner personally. There was a risk they might leave with her departure, impacting revenue predictability.
- **Succession Planning:** As a sole proprietor, the business lacked robust internal systems, with most processes reliant on the owner's direct involvement.

Strategies for Success:

- **Focus on Business Profile:** The owner meticulously documented her candidate sourcing methods, client relationships, and industry expertise - essentially creating a "playbook" for her successor.
- **Warm Introductions for Clients:** She prepared a transition plan for personally introducing key clients to the new owner to facilitate trust and continuity.
- **Limited Consulting Agreement:** The owner negotiated a short-term (6-month) post-sale advisory role to aid with onboarding the new owner.

Outcome

TalentFinders was acquired by a small but growing regional recruitment agency seeking to establish a London presence. The deal terms included:

- An earn-out structure, partially tying the sale price to the retention of major clients over a 12-month period.
- The original owner used her sale proceeds to pursue a graduate degree in a different field, starting an entirely new chapter.
- The acquiring company benefited from TalentFinder's established brand and client base, successfully expanding their geographic reach.

Lessons Learned:

- Documenting processes and relationships is crucial for service businesses where value is tied to the owner's knowledge.
- Buyer fit matters – finding a company that valued the existing client base streamlined the transition.
- Earn-outs can bridge valuation gaps and protect the seller's interests in ensuring client retention post-sale.

Case Study: The Corner Bookshop

- **Industry:** Independent bookstore (focus on children's literature & community events)
- **Location:** Market town, South West England
- **Business Structure:** Family-owned and operated for 15 years
- **Reason for Selling:** Owners, a couple in their late 60s, desiring a slower-paced retirement and more time with grandchildren.

Challenges:

- **Limited Financial Resources:** Small businesses often lack the funds for a dedicated business broker or extensive pre-sale preparations.
- **Local Market Saturation:** The rise of online booksellers posed increasing competition and shrinking profit margins.
- **Legacy Preservation:** The bookshop was a beloved community hub, and the owners were deeply concerned about maintaining its ethos and character under new ownership.

Strategies for Success:

- **Community Outreach:** The owners used local newspapers and their loyal customer base to spread the word about the sale, emphasising their desire to find a buyer passionate about preserving the shop's spirit.
- **Highlight Intangibles:** The business profile showcased the shop's cosy atmosphere, curated selection, and popular children's storytime events as value drivers beyond mere inventory.
- **Creative Deal Structure:** The owners were open to partial seller financing to attract a wider pool of potential buyers, especially those who might lack substantial upfront capital.

Outcome

The Corner Bookshop was purchased by a young teacher with a love for children's literature and prior experience in event planning. The deal involved:

- The previous owners providing mentorship for the first six months, aided by the seller financing agreement.
- Commitment from the new owner to continue the shop's core community events and build on them with fresh ideas.
- The original owners, feeling satisfied passing the torch, successfully transitioned to a happy retirement with the occasional joyful visit to "their" bookshop's bustling story hours.

Lessons Learned:

- Passion can be a currency: Small business sales often attract ideal buyers primarily driven by a love for the business itself rather than just profit potential.
- Seller financing can widen the buyer pool and facilitate the transfer of a cherished local business.
- Finding a buyer aligned with a business's community ethos can be paramount for ensuring a smooth and emotionally fulfilling transition for the seller.

Conclusion: Your Strategy for a Successful Exit

Selling your business is a journey, not just a single transaction. By carefully considering the decisions at each stage – from those first thoughts of a potential sale through to your life after the handover – you maximise both the financial outcome and your personal fulfilment.

I hope this book will help you start on this journey. We've covered the practicalities of valuation, taxation, negotiation, and deal structure. We've delved into the equally important emotional side of letting go of a business you've built, alongside strategies to rediscover your purpose after the sale.

Remember, knowledge is power. Whether you plan to sell your business in the near future or simply wish to ensure it's always "sale-ready," the principles within these chapters set you up for success.

Key Takeaways

- Proactive planning leads to better outcomes than rushed decisions triggered by external circumstances.
- Your business is worth more than its bottom line – intangible assets, like your reputation and your staff's expertise, are valuable currency.
- Seek expert advice. Tax specialists, solicitors, and potentially brokers, are investments in maximising your returns and minimising future headaches.
- Selling isn't the end of your story; it's the start of an exciting new chapter!

A Call to Action

Begin with the end in mind:

- If a sale is a long-term possibility, start streamlining operations, organising documentation, and exploring your personal post-business goals now.
- If a sale is more imminent, assemble your team of advisors and evaluate your options.
- Wherever you are on this journey, use the resources in this book and its appendices to seek further guidance and support.

Selling the business you've poured your heart and soul into is monumental. By approaching it strategically, thoughtfully, and without fear, you open the doors to a future filled with new possibilities, financial security, and the well-deserved pride of knowing you built something of lasting value.

If you've come this far and would like to know more, or would like some advice - my contact details are below - please drop me an email and I look forward to connecting.

Craig Bartlett

https://craigbartlett.com / craig@craigbartlett.com
https://proactivebusinessbrokers.com / craig@proactivebusinessbrokers.com
https://thewealthyexitmethod.com / craig@thewealthyexitmethod.com
LinkedIn: https://linkedin.com/in/craigbartlett1

Printed in Poland
by Amazon Fulfillment
Poland Sp. z o.o., Wrocław

33359068R00018